THE USBORNE
TITANIC
PICTURE BOOK

Megan Cullis & Emily Bone
Illustrated by Ian McNee

Designed by Stephen Moncrieff
& Tom Lalonde

Consultant: Paul Louden-Brown

CONTENTS

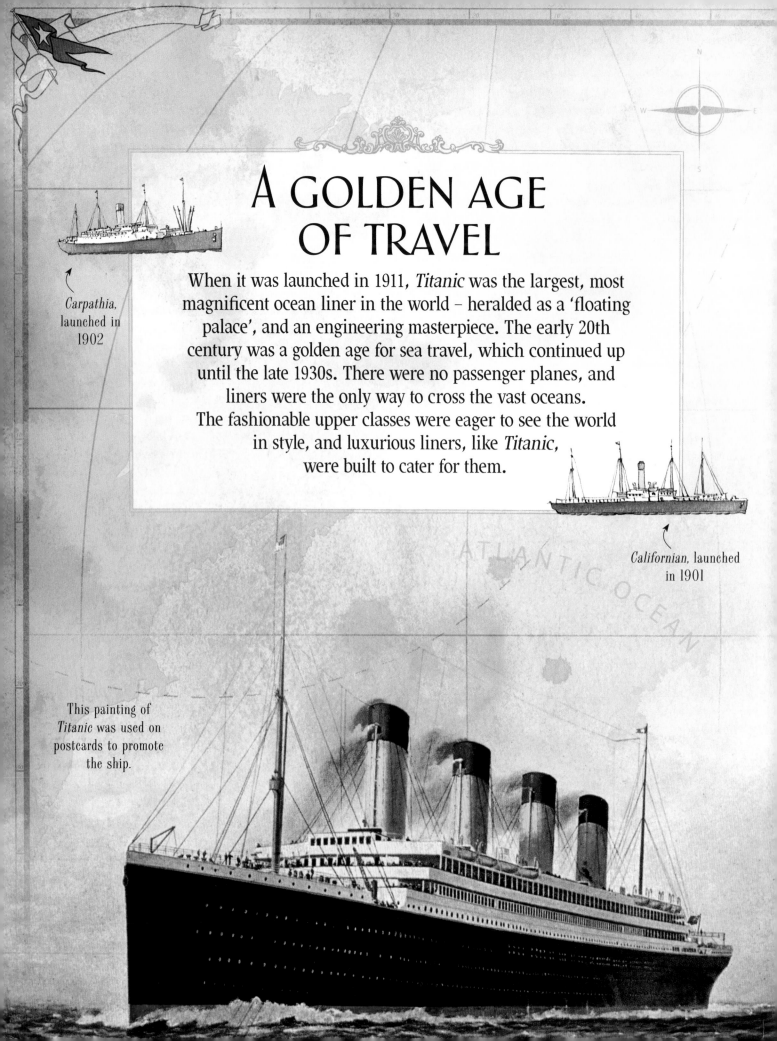

A GOLDEN AGE OF TRAVEL

When it was launched in 1911, *Titanic* was the largest, most magnificent ocean liner in the world – heralded as a 'floating palace', and an engineering masterpiece. The early 20th century was a golden age for sea travel, which continued up until the late 1930s. There were no passenger planes, and liners were the only way to cross the vast oceans.
The fashionable upper classes were eager to see the world in style, and luxurious liners, like *Titanic*, were built to cater for them.

Carpathia, launched in 1902

Californian, launched in 1901

This painting of *Titanic* was used on postcards to promote the ship.

The most advanced ocean liners soon became symbols of national pride. This cover for a children's book of the time captures the excitement surrounding the departure of *Olympic* — the sister ship of *Titanic* — from Southampton.

Stylish customers often drove to the ports. At that time, cars were a novelty that only the wealthiest could afford. Vehicles, like this 1912 French *Renault*, were sometimes transported in the liners' cargo holds.

To transport their expensive belongings, many first-class ticket holders took dozens of trunks with them. Edith Russell — a passenger on *Titanic* — joked, "My luggage is worth more to me than I am."

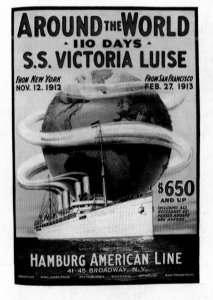

Shipping companies began to take advantage of their exclusive appeal, offering new and exotic travel destinations. This poster advertises around the world cruises with *Hamburg American Line*.

Clothing manufacturers were quick to catch on to the trend for luxury travel. This advertisement for Aquascutum shows its range of overcoats for women, suitable for race, sporting, and steamer travel. The new styles promise 'perfect freedom in any position'.

Millionaires, socialites, celebrities and aristocrats all mingled on board the ocean liners in their finest clothes, celebrating their fortunes and successes. New friendships were formed, and business contacts were made on these society excursions across the seas.

RIVALRY AT SEA

White Star Line

Cunard Line

At the beginning of the 20th century, two shipping companies, the *Cunard Line* and the *White Star Line*, were in fierce competition with each other. Operating between Europe and America, both companies vied to make their ships bigger and better than anyone else's.

In 1907, Lusitania captured the 'Blue Riband' award for crossing the Atlantic in 4 days, 19 hours and 52 minutes. It held the record for the next 22 years.

In 1907, the *Cunard Line* introduced two new ocean liners: *Lusitania* and *Mauretania*. They both held the 'Blue Riband' — an unofficial award that was given to passenger ships that broke the record for crossing the Atlantic Ocean in the fastest time. English newspapers nicknamed the ships the 'greyhounds of the seas' because they were so fast.

LUSITANIA

Passengers: 2,198
Top speed: 25.65 knots
Length: 240m (787ft)

MAURETANIA

Passengers: 2,165
Top speed: 26.06 knots
Length: 241m (790ft)

At the time it was built, *Mauretania* was the largest passenger liner in the world.

The main lounge and library inside *Mauretania* were designed in the style of the Palace of Versailles.

In 1913, Britain's King George V and Queen Mary were given a special tour of *Mauretania*, further adding to the prestige of the liner.

A *Cunard Line* poster advertising sailing times to New York and Boston

LARGEST STEAMERS IN THE WORLD

Determined not to be outdone, the *White Star Line* commissioned three 'Olympic-class' liners — *Olympic, Titanic* and *Britannic*. Intended to beat *Mauretania* and *Lusitania* in luxury rather than speed, the ships aimed to cross the Atlantic in about five and a half days.

Titanic was known as RMS *Titanic*. RMS stands for 'Royal Mail Steamer'. It was contracted to carry British and US mail.

The Olympic-class liners offered the ultimate in luxurious travel for people crossing the Atlantic.

TITANIC & OLYMPIC

Passengers:
  Titanic 3,547
  Olympic 2,435
Top speed: 23 knots
Length: 269m (883ft)

This photograph shows *Titanic* (right) and *Olympic* (left) in the Belfast dock in Northern Ireland, just after they had been built. Their sister ship, *Britannic*, was launched three years later, in 1914.

WHITE STAR LINE R.M.S "OLYMPIC"
COMPARED WITH VARIOUS FAMOUS BUILDINGS.

As this postcard shows, if balanced at one end, the liners would tower over the world's tallest buildings — the Woolworth Building, New York (fifth from left) and St. Peter's, Rome, Italy (right).

NAUTICAL TERMS

Nautical mile: 1.85km (1.15 miles)

Knot: A unit of speed equivalent to 1 nautical mile per hour.

Hull: The main body of a ship.

Port: The left-hand side of a ship facing forward.

Starboard: The right-hand side of a ship facing forward.

Bow: The front of a ship.

Stern: The rear part of a ship.

Helm: The ship's wheel used for steering.

BUILDING TITANIC

Shipbuilders *Harland & Wolff* started work on *Titanic* in the spring of 1909, ordered by the *White Star Line* to build the ship 'barring no expense'. The ship's construction took 15,000 men over two years to complete.

Harland & Wolff shipyard in Belfast, Northern Ireland, had large slipways in which the enormous steel hull was constructed. The shipyard had the tallest gantries (overhead cranes) in the world to lift the heavy steel plates.

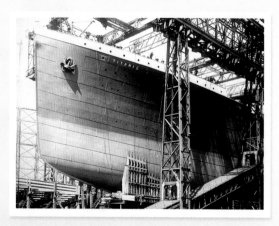

A frame was built, then heavy steel plates were secured to it with three million rivets. The hull was 268m (882ft) long — as long as 40 buses.

Titanic was big news. Newspapers from around the world sent 'special correspondents' to report every stage of the ship's construction.

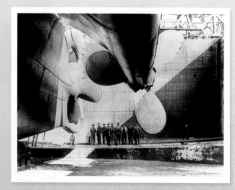

The engines turned three huge propellers that were fitted to the stern (back) of *Titanic*. They powered the ship through the water.

Workers followed a 9m (32ft) long blueprint (master plan) while building the ship. You can see below how the ship was made up of 16 watertight compartments. The theory was that if the hull was damaged, water would only flow into one or two compartments, and the ship would stay afloat.

Lifeboats: only 20 ended up on ship as designers didn't want to clutter up the decks.

Cranes for lifting passenger luggage on board

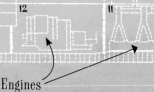

Propellers (the third is on the other side of the ship)

16 15 14 13 12 11 10 9

Stern

Watertight compartments: numbered 1-16, marked on the diagram by thick white lines.

Engines

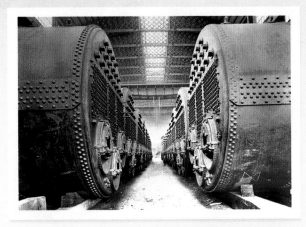

Inside the hull, 29 massive coal-fired boilers were built to make the steam to power the engines. Over 700,000kg (1,500,000lbs) of coal was fed into the furnaces every day and burned to keep the ship moving.

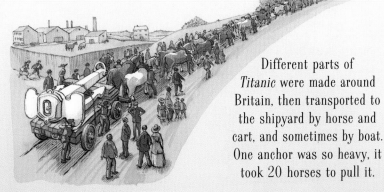

Different parts of *Titanic* were made around Britain, then transported to the shipyard by horse and cart, and sometimes by boat. One anchor was so heavy, it took 20 horses to pull it.

Funnels: *Titanic* had three working funnels. A fourth, dummy funnel was added at the back to make the ship look more powerful. It was also used to store coal.

THE LAUNCH

At 12:13pm on May 31, 1911, *Titanic* was launched for the first time. The slipways were greased using 20,000kg (44,000lbs) of oil and soap, and it took just 62 seconds for the ship to slip into the water.

A crowd of 100,000 gathered, excited to catch a glimpse of the completed hull. They shouted "There she goes!" as the biggest ship ever built sailed out into the River Lagan, Belfast.

Launch

OF

White Star Royal Mail Triple-Screw Steamer

"TITANIC"

At BELFAST,

Wednesday, 31st May, 1911, at 12-15 p.m.

Admit Bearer.

A ticket to the launch

Rigging

Crow's nest (lookout)

8   7   6   5   4   3   2   1

Boilers

Coal bunkers: there was a bunker next to each boiler.

Bow

FIXTURES AND FITTINGS

Once the hull was complete, a new team of designers and craftsmen set to work fitting the interior of *Titanic*. It took ten months to transform it into a stunning floating hotel, with ten decks, state-of-the-art facilities, and luxurious rooms.

First-class passengers would enter the ship through a grand 18m (60ft) wooden staircase. Ornate clocks, specially commissioned paintings and elaborately carved bannisters adorned the staircase. It was designed to be an elegant meeting place where passengers could gather before lunch and dinner. A beautiful glass dome was fitted at the top of the grand staircase to let in natural light.

This is an illustration of the grand staircase from a *White Star Line* brochure.

Impressive chandeliers were used to light up first-class communal areas and lounges. Each one was made to sparkle with up to 50 electric bulbs.

Companies were eager to supply *White Star Line* ships, as they were known for the high quality of their fixtures and fittings. Here a glass light manufacturer, *Perry & Co.*, is using the fact that they supplied lamps and chandeliers for *Titanic* in their advertising, so customers associate the company with such a glamorous ship.

Bronze sculptures, such as this cherub that stood at the foot of the grand staircase, were designed to hold elegant lamps that would light up the ship's corridors in the evenings.

All kinds of items were specially commissioned for use on *Titanic* and branded by *White Star Line*. The company logo was printed onto everything, from stationery to tableware, to prove how exclusive these items were.

Passengers were given luggage labels with the *White Star* logo printed on them. The idea was that after the journey, the labels could be kept as mementos.

These eggcups were used during breakfast service in the first-class dining room.

Harland & Wolff brought hundreds of designers and craftsmen to their workshops in Belfast to produce hand-crafted interior decor for their ships.

Luxurious communal rooms were furnished with thick-pile carpets, silk tapestries and fine wood furniture. First-class reception rooms, like this one, were decorated with intricate plasterwork on the ceiling as well as etched glass panels.

Titanic had the very latest technology, including electric fires. They were built inside traditional fireplaces, like the one in this photograph on the left.

While the ship was being decorated, local artisans came on board, hoping *Harland & Wolff* would buy their products. This woman above is selling her lacework.

For the very first time on a ship, electric lifts took passengers between floors.

THE MAIDEN VOYAGE

On April 10, 1912, *Titanic* set off on its first voyage from Southampton, England, heading for New York, USA. Weeks before its departure, preparations were underway to get the steamship ready to go to sea.

On April 2, *Titanic* was tugged out to sea from its dock in Belfast. After the engines, steering gear and other equipment were checked, the ship was ready to steam on to Southampton to prepare for its first journey across the North Atlantic.

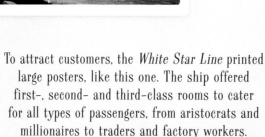

To attract customers, the *White Star Line* printed large posters, like this one. The ship offered first-, second- and third-class rooms to cater for all types of passengers, from aristocrats and millionaires to traders and factory workers.

A third-class ticket, like this one, cost around £8 — about £380 ($600) today. Most of the 709 third-class passengers were making one-way journeys, emigrating to America.

Second-class tickets cost slightly more at £12 — about £580 ($900) today.

There were 325 first-class passengers on *Titanic*. The price of this first-class ticket was around £945, which is about £45,400 ($71,300) in today's money.

The wealthiest passenger on board was the American tycoon John Jacob Astor. With him was his wife, Madeleine, and their dog, Kitty.

STANDARD LIFE JACKET.

1st Position.   2nd Position.   3rd Position.

DIRECTIONS FOR USE.

1.—Place the Jacket over the head passing the arms through the armholes. It will slip over the head easier if the hollow shape of the back pocket is first placed against the back of the neck and the front then drawn down over the head.

2.—Tie a half knot with the tapes in front. Draw them well tight.

3.—And complete knot.

THIS JACKET IS REVERSIBLE, AND ONLY THE TAPES IN FRONT NEED BE TIED.

These instructions were displayed inside the ship to demonstrate how to use the life jackets in an emergency.

On the morning of departure, the 885 members of the crew took their places on the ship, while a Board of Trade Inspector examined the life jackets and lifeboats.

At 9:30, the *Titanic Special* — a train from London Waterloo — arrived at Southampton, and the first passengers streamed on board.

At 12:00 noon, *Titanic* left Southampton docks, with 2,201 people on board. As the ship pulled away, some passengers stood out on deck, waving goodbye to their families and friends.

Before crossing the North Atlantic, *Titanic* stopped to pick up passengers and mail from Cherbourg, France, and Queenstown, Ireland. These Irish emigrants are waiting to board at Queenstown.

PLANNED ROUTE

This map shows the route *Titanic* was scheduled to take to America. It was due to arrive in New York on April 17, 1912.

BELFAST

QUEENSTOWN

SOUTHAMPTON

CHERBOURG

NEW YORK

Titanic was too big to dock at Cherbourg and Queenstown, so small boats called tenders ferried passengers and mail to the ship.

STAFF ON TITANIC

The *White Star Line* prided itself on the experience of its crew and the level of service it offered. As the largest liner afloat, *Titanic* needed a large and capable team. The ship left Southampton with 885 employees on board.

The captain, Edward James Smith, had over 40 years' experience commanding large passenger liners. As well as giving orders about the course and speed of the ship, he also entertained and dined with important passengers.

First Officer William Murdoch and Second Officer Charles Lightoller led the deck crew. They were responsible for steering and navigating the ship.

Lookouts were part of the deck crew. They worked high up in the crow's nest, looking out for hazards, such as other ships and icebergs.

Officers with Captain Smith (6th from right) on the deck of *Titanic*.

STEWARDS

Stewards made up the largest section of staff. They were on hand at all times to attend to passengers' calls.

First-class steward's badge

Each steward was assigned to first, second, or third class. All stewards were easily distinguished by their badges.

Titanic had an advanced wireless radio system that could send messages up to 400km (250 miles) away. Operators Jack Phillips and Harold Bride worked long hours sending hundreds of messages each day.

Musicians played to passengers in the lounge areas while they were dining. They knew 352 tunes by heart.

Postal workers had the task of sorting the 3,364 bags of mail that were brought on ship, as well as dealing with any letters posted on board by passengers and crew. They worked in a designated mail room, like this one below.

Firemen worked in scorching heat in the very bottom of the ship, stoking the furnaces with coal to keep the ship moving 24 hours a day.

With sophisticated electrical systems throughout the ship, staff were on hand to fix any problems. Electricians walked around the ship every few hours, making sure that all lights were working. Some had keys to every room.

This is Samuel E. Hemming. He checked that interior and exterior lights were working on *Titanic*.

Just two window cleaners made sure each of the ship's 3,000 windows was spotless.

LUXURY LIVING

From luxurious first-class suites with private promenades, to basic but comfortable six-person cabins for third-class passengers, staying on board was designed to be a pleasurable experience for all.

This is a first-class bedroom in the style of Louis XVI — a lavish style inspired by 18th-century French palaces.

One first-class passenger wrote in a letter, "Our rooms are furnished in the best of taste and most luxuriously, and they are really rooms, not cabins." Each suite was beautifully decorated in one of nine period styles.

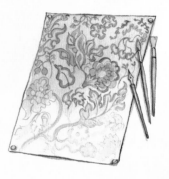

Elegant wallpaper patterns were designed specially for the ship.

Steward call bells were fixed in every room, so passengers could summon stewards 24 hours a day.

This Regency (19th-century) style sitting room is part of an expensive suite that cost £870 to stay in (£40,000 or $65,000 today). It was nicknamed the 'millionaire suite'.

Adjoining sitting rooms allowed passengers to take tea in their rooms, or retreat in the evenings for after-dinner games and drinks. This woman is writing letters at a writing desk in her cabin.

Some suites had private sheltered promenades so that passengers could walk on the deck without the discomfort of cold, Atlantic winds.

WHERE DID PASSENGERS STAY?

The majority of space on board was reserved for first-class passengers, across 39 suites and 350 cabins. Cabins for 550 second-class passengers were situated at either end of the ship. Up to 1,000 third-class passengers stayed in communal cabins, mostly on the lower decks of the ship.

First class   Second class   Third class

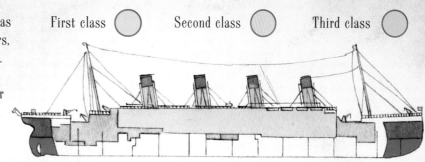

All passengers had access to toilet and washing facilities. First-class suites had a bathroom with a large bathtub, washbasin and hot and cold running water. Some even had a shower, too. This is an illustration of a first-class bathroom from a *White Star Line* brochure.

First-class passengers without a private bathroom used public facilities that had to be booked in advance. A bath steward would run a bath and call the passenger when it was ready.

Rooms for second-class passengers were equivalent to first-class on other liners. Second-class cabins could accommodate one to four people, and had washbasins that folded away when not being used.

A sofa allowed passengers to relax in their rooms.

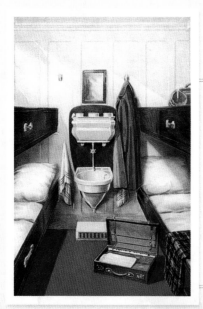

Sharing cabins with up to five other people, a third-class passenger could expect fresh drinking water delivered daily, and warm blankets on the beds. On other ships of the time, passengers had to bring their own bed linen.

This third-class cabin has a washbasin between the beds.

With only two third-class bathrooms on *Titanic*, passengers often had to go up or down a deck to reach them.

FINE DINING

With a choice of two cafés, a dining saloon and a restaurant, *Titanic* offered first-class passengers a dining experience more lavish than many of the best restaurants on land. Second- and third-class passengers were also well provided for.

Breakfast, lunch and dinner were served in the ship's dining saloons. The first-class saloon, as shown in this photograph, was decorated in a 'style particularly English', with oak furniture and an ornate carpet.

A first-class dinner consisted of eleven courses, served every evening at 7pm. The menu included mutton cutlets, fillet of veal, and French ice cream for dessert. Food was sourced from all over the world.

First-class passengers would usually meet in the reception room before dinner. They were expected to wear formal attire — dinner suits for men, and evening dresses for women.

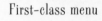

First-class menu

Second-class menu

Diners in second class were offered a choice of four main courses, followed by a selection of desserts.

For a more intimate dining experience, first-class passengers could eat at the *Café Parisien*, enjoying views of the sea as they ate. The menu included roast duckling, oysters and chocolate éclairs. This photograph is from a *White Star Line* brochure.

Meals in first and second class were served on beautifully decorated bone china. This plate from first class is edged with real gold.

In the second-class dining saloon, passengers were seated on mahogany furniture. A pianist played light music to accompany their meal.

Chefs on board the ship prepared around 10,000 meals a day. As well as having two enormous galleys (kitchens), *Titanic* was also equipped with two bakeries and two butcheries.

A team of cooks specialized in preparing different types of food. These included pastry cooks who baked hundreds of pies and tarts every day.

Before leaving England, *Titanic* was stocked with 1,500 bottles of wine, 20,000 bottles of beer and stout, and 850 bottles of spirits.

Many of the drinks, side dishes and desserts were served in elegant crystal glassware, like this.

Third-class menu

Meals in third class were simpler, with dishes including boiled potatoes, ham and eggs or roast beef. But for many third-class passengers, it might have been the best food they'd ever tasted.

Titanic had two third-class dining saloons. They were painted in plain white, but they were comfortable and well lit.

ACTIVITIES ON BOARD

All sorts of diversions were offered on board, including a gym, a swimming pool and luxury Turkish baths. Some of the facilities were the first of their kind to be provided on a ship.

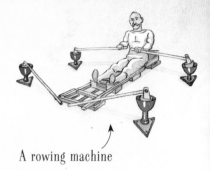

A rowing machine

First-class passengers could visit a state-of-the-art gym, open to men, women and children at different times of day. The *White Star Line* claimed passengers could, 'obtain beneficial exercise, besides endless amusement'.

An exercise bike

Electric horse machines allowed passengers to simulate the action of riding a horse.

The Turkish baths, illustrated here, included heated rooms and a steam room, decorated with traditional Turkish-style tiles. There was also a new invention to try — electric beds that heated the body with lamps.

Bathers could use a special weighing chair to compare their weight before and after a visit to the baths.

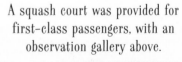

A squash court was provided for first-class passengers, with an observation gallery above.

Titanic was one of the first ever ships to have a swimming pool on board. The pool was filled with heated sea water, and was only available to first-class passengers. This illustration of the pool is from a *White Star Line* brochure.

This is a photograph of the Georgian-style reading and writing room, where first-class passengers could relax in a quiet atmosphere.

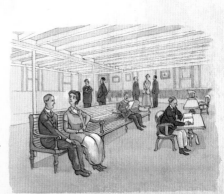

Packs of playing cards, branded with the *White Star Line* logo, were available for after-dinner games in the smoking room.

On the first- and second-class decks, passengers could play games such as shuffleboard or bull board. White markings that were required for a game were chalked on the wooden deck by a deck steward.

First-class passengers were allowed to bring pet dogs on the voyage. In return for a half-fare ticket, dogs were held in luxury kennels and kept well fed by the ship's butcher.

The young boy in this photograph is playing with a spinning top.

This painting shows passengers enjoying the afternoon sunshine on the second-class deck.

A general room was provided for the third-class passengers. It acted as a nursery, lounge and social area.

ICEBERG, RIGHT AHEAD!

On Sunday, April 14 at 11:40pm, one of the lookouts spotted an iceberg in the ship's path. Just 37 seconds later, the ship collided with it, and holes were ripped into the hull. Distress calls were sent out and nearby ships raced to help.

This map shows the position of ships on the night of the disaster and how far they were from *Titanic*.

ICE FIELD

RMS TITANIC

The freezing cold North Atlantic Ocean is littered with icebergs. They're hard to spot because most of an iceberg is underwater.

MOUNT TEMPLE
80KM (50 MILES)

Received distress call from *Titanic* but had incorrect coordinates and became cut off by ice field. Arrived late.

PARISIAN
80KM (50 MILES)

Unable to reach *Titanic* in time due to the dangerous ice field, but helped to direct other ships in the area.

BIRMA
113KM (70 MILES)

First to receive distress messages. Prepared for rescue, but was given incorrect coordinates.

FRANKFURT
225KM (140 MILES)

Frankfurt was over eight hours away from *Titanic* when the radio operators received the ship's distress call. Arrived late.

CANADA

USA

This is where *Titanic* hit the iceberg in the Atlantic Ocean. The ship was almost three-quarters of its way through the journey.

IRELAND

UK

1,100km (680 miles) to New York

3,400km (2,100 miles) from Queenstown (Ireland)

Throughout the day, radio operators Jack Phillips and Harold Bride received messages from other ships warning of large icebergs in the area. But the captain ordered the ship to continue, regardless.

11:00pm Iceberg warning sent from nearby ship, SS *Californian* to *Titanic*: "We are stopped and surrounded by ice." Ignored by *Titanic* radio operators, as they are too busy sending a backlog of passenger messages.

11:40pm Frederick Fleet, one of the lookouts, spots a huge iceberg right in front of *Titanic*. He doesn't see it until the last minute because the binoculars had been left behind when the ship docked in Southampton.

He rings the ship's bell three times, and telephones the officer steering the ship, shouting, "Iceberg, right ahead!"

First officer William Murdoch orders his crew to shut down engines and steer the ship hard to port (to the left).

11:40:37pm *Titanic* hits the iceberg. Several steel plates on the starboard (right) side of the hull are twisted and broken.

The hull is made up of 16 compartments, with watertight doors sealing each one. The ship is designed to stay afloat even if two compartments are flooded.

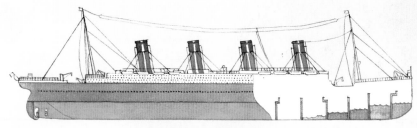

Water enters five compartments and quickly flows into more. Thomas Andrews, who helped design *Titanic*, is on board to advise. He calculates that the ship has two hours until it sinks.

11:45pm First distress messages sent out by Phillips and Bride.

This is the message. Cqd means "All stations alert! Distress!" M.G.Y is the ship's identification code.

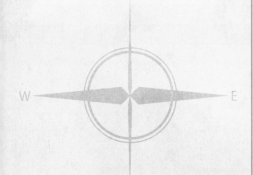

12:05am Distress flares are fired. Captain Smith orders lifeboats to be uncovered and filled with passengers.

CALIFORNIAN
16KM (10 MILES)

The closest ship to *Titanic*. Passengers reported seeing its lights in the distance. *Titanic* sent messages to the ship, but the radio operator had gone to bed and never received them.

CARPATHIA
93KM (58 MILES)

Responded to the distress call, but would take three hours to reach the ship. Despite this, it was the first to arrive at the site.

ABANDON SHIP

When *Titanic* hit the iceberg, most passengers only felt a slight shiver. Orders were given to abandon ship, but many refused to believe that the so-called unsinkable ship was sinking and were reluctant to leave. Only when it started to tilt did panic set in.

Staff calmly prepared passengers for evacuation, and lifeboats were swung out from the boat deck. But, out of 2,201 people on board, there was only enough space in the lifeboats for 1,178.

With no idea of the danger they were in, children played with the chunks of ice that had fallen on the deck as *Titanic* hit the iceberg.

Officers commanded, "Women and children first!" before helping them into boats. Men were only allowed on as oarsmen, or if there were no women nearby. Passengers were scared to leave the warmth and light of the ship for the freezing, pitch-black ocean.

At 12:45am, the first lifeboat, Lifeboat 7, was lowered, with only 28 passengers, out of a total capacity of 65. Further lifeboats were lowered, less than half filled.

This artist's impression of lifeboats being lowered was published by a newspaper two weeks after *Titanic* sank.

Father Thomas Byles, a Catholic priest, stayed on the deck reciting prayers and hearing passengers' confessions. He twice refused a place in a lifeboat.

Musicians played to keep passengers' spirits up. Their last song before the ship sank was said to be the hymn 'Nearer, my God, to thee'. Newspaper articles, like this one (left), compared them to men on the *Birkenhead* — a famous ship that sank while the officers bravely stayed on deck, helping to save women and children.

When the front of
Titanic started to dip,
people became really
nervous. More than 70
people crowded onto
Lifeboat 11, one of the
last to be lowered.
Some jumped into the
freezing sea hoping to
be picked up later.

Those in third class found it difficult to reach
the boat deck, as their rooms were several decks
below. A few brave stewards went down into the
sinking ship to guide passengers to the lifeboats.

By 2:05am, all the lifeboats had been
launched. Passengers lucky enough to have a
space in a boat had to wait for rescue. Some
boats went back to pick up any survivors
in the sea, but most stayed put. People
were scared of lifeboats being swamped by
survivors trying to climb in.

This is one of only 49
life buoys on *Titanic*.
Even if passengers
managed to grab hold of
a life buoy, they would
only be able to survive
30 minutes in the -2°C
(28°F) water.

Frederick Fleet, the lookout who first spotted
the iceberg, is in the front of this lifeboat.

Harold Bride and Jack Phillips worked until the last
minute sending distress telegrams. They escaped by
clinging to an upturned lifeboat.

At around 2:20am, the ship's bow
suddenly sank, sending the stern into
the air and exposing the propellers.
People floating in lifeboats watched
helplessly as the ship plunged into the
water. Captain Smith and First Officer
William Murdoch were still on board,
along with almost 1,500 passengers.

One survivor sketched this — his
impression of how the ship sank, from
hitting the iceberg at 11:45pm, to
sinking at around 2:00am.

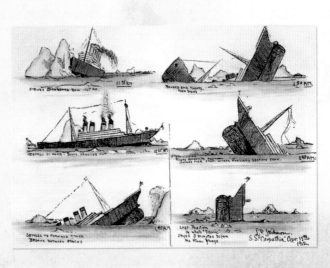

CARPATHIA TO THE RESCUE

At 12:30am, *Titanic* sent out the distress call, "SOS Titanic sinking by the head. We are about all down. Sinking..." On receiving the message, the passenger liner *Carpathia* raced at full speed, dashing through ice fields to reach the site of the disaster.

Aboard *Carpathia*, Captain Rostron ordered for the ship's heating and hot water to be switched off. Every bit of steam from the boilers was needed to help power the engines so the ship could reach *Titanic* as quickly as possible.

The crew frantically collected warm clothes and blankets, and made hot soup and drinks ready for the survivors. They were told to drink lots of coffee to prepare for the long night ahead.

It wasn't until 4:10am that the crew on *Carpathia* spotted the first lifeboat. They immediately dropped down rope ladders so the survivors could climb aboard. Sacks and cargo nets were lowered to pull up children and less agile people.

Over the next four hours, 711 survivors were taken on board *Carpathia*. Survivors huddled together on the deck with blankets, desperately trying to get warm.

When it became clear there was no one left to save, *Carpathia* headed back to New York. Shortly after, Canadian ships *SS Mackay-Bennett*, *Minia*, *Montmagny* and *Algerine* arrived to collect the bodies. There were too many to take them all back to land, so many were buried at sea. The rest were taken to Halifax, Novia Scotia, where headstones would later be put up by the *White Star Line*.

News spread fast across the world that *Titanic* had sunk. Shocking headlines filled the news stands — the one in this photograph reads: TITANIC DISASTER GREAT LOSS OF LIFE. The world waited tensely for the survivors' return, eager to hear the story.

It wasn't until the evening of April 18 that *Carpathia* finally arrived in New York. Over 30,000 people lined the docks, including hordes of journalists, medics and government officials, waiting to catch the first glimpses of the harrowed survivors.

Injured survivors were carefully helped off *Carpathia* by doctors. This photograph shows Harold Bride, wireless operator of *Titanic*, with his frostbitten feet wrapped in bandages.

REWARDING BRAVERY

Soon after their return, the members of *Carpathia* were awarded medals for their rescue efforts. Captain Rostron was given a silver cup and gold medal, and later the Congressional Medal of Honor in gold — the highest civilian award in the USA.

THE AFTERMATH

The disaster was front-page news on newspapers across the world for weeks after the sinking. Everyone demanded to know who was accountable. Meanwhile, survivors and families of those who died had to come to terms with the terrible tragedy.

This picture shows crowds gathering at the *White Star Line* offices in London, including relatives of *Titanic* passengers desperate for news.

When they arrived in New York, many survivors were alone, scared and penniless. The majority boarded a ship back to England, but some set up a new life in the USA and Canada.

Inquiries into the sinking were held in New York and London. The first started on April 19, when J. Bruce Ismay, the managing director of the *White Star Line*, was questioned. He escaped *Titanic* on a lifeboat, and was branded a coward for not going down with the ship.

J. Bruce Ismay (on the right) arriving at the New York inquiry with his attorney

The ship's design, journey and collision were scrutinized at the inquiries. All survivors were interviewed.

This photograph was taken at the New York inquiry. Big plans of the ship were drawn up so witnesses could easily explain how they escaped the ship. The inquiries concluded that significant safety improvements, such as lifeboats for all passengers, would have prevented such a great loss of life.

As well as covering the inquiries, newspapers were filled with stories imagining the final moments of *Titanic*. This front page from the *Daily Sketch* features a picture of Captain Smith on the deck with the headline: "Where the British Captain stood 'til death."

When the ship sank, some passengers lost everything they owned. Newspapers ran campaigns encouraging the public to give money to those in need.

Each family received a form, like this, telling them of their relative's death. Families of those who died had often lost their sole breadwinner. The Titanic Relief Fund was set up by the British government to give a weekly payment to those families.

On April 23, 1912, a memorial boat carrying relatives and friends sailed out to the site where *Titanic* sank. Prayers were said, and flowers scattered on the water.

The *Titanic* story affected many who heard it. People were moved to send mourning postcards as an indication of their grief. This one includes the name of the last song the band is said to have played on deck before the ship went down.

LOST OR SAVED

Out of 2,201 people on board *Titanic*, only 711 survived.

First-class passengers
Survived: 203   Died: 122

Second-class passengers
Survived: 118   Died: 167

Third-class passengers
Survived: 178   Died: 528

Staff and crew
Survived: 212   Died: 673

Memorials to the victims were built in Belfast, Southampton, Liverpool, London, Halifax, Nova Scotia and other cities around the world. Even today, people lay flowers and wreaths to remember those who died.

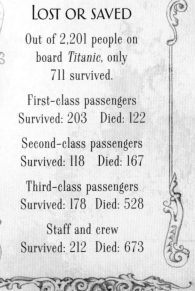

Passenger stories

In the aftermath of the *Titanic* disaster, stories unfolded of the courage shown by the survivors, and of the many people who had sacrificed their lives for others.

Margaret 'Molly' Brown
⟷ 1ST CLASS ⟷

Margaret Brown, an American human rights activist, escaped on Lifeboat 6 and helped to row the boat to safety. She also inspired the other women to row, while keeping their spirits up with stories and songs. On *Carpathia*, she established the Survivors' Committee to help raise money for the survivors who were left penniless after the disaster.

In 1960, the story of Margaret Brown's life was turned into a musical show entitled, *The Unsinkable Molly Brown*.

Benjamin Guggenheim
⟷ 1ST CLASS ⟷

Benjamin Guggenheim, a wealthy American businessman, drowned. After helping his mistress and her maid into a lifeboat, he and his valet changed into their evening clothes. He was heard saying, "We're dressed up in our best and are prepared to go down like gentlemen."

Guggenheim and his valet were last seen sipping brandy and smoking cigars.

The Duff-Gordons
⟷ 1ST CLASS ⟷

Lady Duff-Gordon, a British fashion designer, was on her way to New York with her husband, Cosmo, and her secretary, Laura Francatelli. All three managed to escape on Lifeboat 1, with only nine others on board. Later, the Duff-Gordons were accused of bribing the lifeboat crew not to go back to rescue more people, but this was found to be untrue.

Cosmo Duff-Gordon gave the lifeboat crew members £5 ($8) each to help compensate for their personal losses on *Titanic*.

This floral afternoon gown was designed by Lady Duff-Gordon's fashion house, *Lucile Ltd*. The company designed luxury clothes for many famous clients, including actors, singers and even royalty.

Edith Rosenbaum Russell
1st Class

US fashion journalist Edith Russell was returning to New York from Paris on *Titanic*. She refused to jump into Lifeboat 11 unless her lucky pig was thrown in first — a furry toy that played music. Edith was later rescued by *Carpathia*, along with her toy.

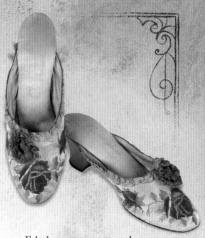

While waiting to be rescued, her musical pig was used to entertain the children.

Edith was wearing these embroidered slippers when she climbed into the lifeboat.

Michel and Edmond Navratil
2nd Class

These two French brothers were nicknamed 'the *Titanic* orphans' because for a while after the disaster, no one knew who they were. Their identities were eventually discovered, and they were reunited with their mother. The boys had been kidnapped by their father, who died on *Titanic*.

Newspapers published the boys' pictures to try to find out who they were.

Lillian Asplund
3rd Class

Lillian Asplund, a five-year-old American girl, boarded *Titanic* with her parents and four brothers. On the night of the disaster, Lillian was put into a lifeboat with her mother and younger brother, but the rest of her family was left behind. Lillian sat between her mother's knees in the lifeboat to keep warm. She later compared *Titanic* to a 'big building going down'.

This pocket watch was owned by Lillian's father, Carl, who died. The watch is frozen at 4:10am — the time it hit the icy water.

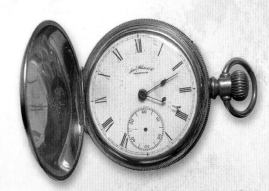

DISCOVERING THE WRECK

For the next 73 years after the disaster, the wreck of *Titanic* remained undiscovered, resting at the bottom of the Atlantic Ocean. It wasn't until 1985 that a team of underwater explorers finally located it, and began to piece together the mystery of how it sank.

TAKING PICTURES

On September 1, 1985, Dr. Robert Ballard, an underwater explorer, found the first signs of the wreck. Sailing out into the Atlantic on the research ship *Knorr*, he used an underwater search vehicle called *Argo* to dive to the sea floor (which was too deep for divers). He took pictures, and sent them back to a ship on the surface.

The wreck of *Titanic* was discovered 21km (13 miles) away from the last recorded position before the ship sank. It was found in two main pieces, indicating that the ship had split as it sank. The bow lies 600m (1,970ft) from the stern on the ocean floor.

Video cameras on *Argo* scanned the sea floor for *Titanic*. After ten days, it captured the very first images, 4km (2.5 miles) below the surface.

A robot attached to *Argo*, named *Jason*, moved in to take close-up pictures. Images from *Jason* and *Argo* were sent back to the ship.

This crystal chandelier was discovered still dangling from its wires, in front of the grand staircase.

Photographs reveal that parts of the wreck remain relatively intact. The ship's starboard propeller — made from very strong bronze — was found broken, but in good condition.

Ever since the wreck was discovered, researchers have been exploring the ship's skeleton inside mini-submarines, or 'subs'. The first human explorations were made in a sub called *Alvin*.

Robotic arms attached to the subs have managed to pick up thousands of items from the wreck. This arm is retrieving a stained glass window.

SALVAGED FROM THE WRECK

Among the recovered items was this leather bag. It was owned by a purser — a member of the ship's crew who was responsible for any valuables on board. The bag had been stuffed with rings and necklaces, probably in the hope that it would be rescued before the ship went down.

In 1998, a team of salvage experts raised a large section of the broken hull. It contained four port holes, and weighed a massive 15,000kg (33,150lb) — the largest part of *Titanic* that has ever been raised. Now known as the 'Big Piece', it is currently on display in an exhibition in Las Vegas, USA.

The fragile remains of *Titanic* are now slowly being broken down by rust-eating bacteria. Scientists predict that over the next 50 years the wreck will become nothing more than a rust stain on the ocean floor. *Titanic* now serves as a quiet and peaceful grave site for all those who died.

INDEX

Usborne Quicklinks

For links to websites with video clips and reconstructions of the *Titanic*, including how it was built, stories from survivors and the discovery and exploration of the wreck, go to the Usborne Quicklinks website at www.usborne.com/quicklinks and type in the keyword 'Titanic'. Please follow the internet safety guidelines at the Usborne Quicklinks website.

Acknowledgements

Every effort has been made to trace and acknowledge ownership of copyright. If any rights have been omitted, the publishers offer to rectify this in any future editions following notification. The publishers are grateful to the following individuals and organizations for their permission to reproduce material on the following pages: t=top, m=middle, b=bottom; r=right, l=left

Cover: © Mary Evans Picture Library/Onslow Auctions Limited (background); ml © Illustrated London News Ltd./Mary Evans (Captain Edward Smith); tr, br, bl © Mary Evans Picture Library/Onslow Auctions Limited (*Olympic* showcard, *Titanic* lifebelt and *Titanic* second-class deck); **p2-3 A golden age of travel**: p2b © Mary Evans Picture Library/Onslow Auctions Limited; p3tl © Titanic: The Ship Magnificent; p3tr © Martin Bennett/Alamy; p3m © Image Courtesy of The Advertising Archives; p3b © Image Courtesy of The Advertising Archives; **p4-5 Rivalry at sea**: p4t © Mary Evans/Rue des Archives/Tallandier; p4b © Mary Evans Picture Library/Onslow Auctions Limited; p5t © Mary Evans Picture Library/Onslow Auctions Limited; p5m, p5b © National Museums Northern Ireland Collection, Harland and Wolff, Ulster Folk and Transport Museum; **p6-7 Building *Titanic***: p6t © Ralph White/Corbis; p6m © World History Archive/Topfoto; p7tl, p7tr © National Museums Northern Ireland Collection, Harland and Wolff, Ulster Folk and Transport Museum; p7m (launch ticket) © Mary Evans Picture Library/Onslow Auctions Limited; p6-7b © The Mariners' Museum/Corbis; **p8-9 Fixtures and fittings**: p8t © Roger-Viollet/Rex Features; p8bl © Paul Louden-Brown/White Star Line Archive Collection; p8br © Barcroft Media via Getty Images; p9tr (eggcups) Photograph by kind permission of Cuttlestones Auctioneers; p9mr (woman selling lace) © Universal Images Group/SuperStock; p9ml, p9bl © Titanic: The Ship Magnificent; **p10-11 The maiden voyage**: p10t © Hulton-Deutsch Collection/Corbis; p10mr (*White Star Line* poster) © Paul Louden-Brown/White Star Line Archive Collection; p10ml (third-class ticket) © 2001 Topham/PressNet/TopFoto; p10b © The Granger Collection/TopFoto; p11t © Paul Louden-Brown/White Star Line Archive Collection; p11m © Universal Images Group/Superstock; **p12-13 Staff on *Titanic***: p12t, p12m, p12b, p13b (keys and Samuel E. Hemming) © Mary Evans Picture Library/Onslow Auctions Limited; p13tl © Illustrated London News Ltd/Mary Evans; p13mr © Mary Evans/Interfoto; p13ml © Titanic: The Ship Magnificent; **p14-15 Luxury living**: p14t, p14m, p14b, p15b © Titanic: The Ship Magnificent; p15ml © National Museums Northern Ireland Collection, Harland and Wolff, Ulster Folk and Transport Museum; p15mr © Mary Evans Picture Library/Onslow Auctions Limited; **p16-17 Fine dining**: p16t © Disney/Everett/Rex Features; p16ml (first-class menu) © Topham/PA/TopFoto; p16mr (second-class menu) © National Maritime Museum, Greenwich, London; p16b © Sipa Press/Rex Features; p17t © Paul Louden-Brown/White Star Line Archive Collection; p17m © Ralph White/Corbis, p17b © TopFoto; **p18-19 Activities on board**: p18t © Illustrated London News Ltd./Mary Evans; p18m, p18b © Mary Evans Picture Library/Onslow Auctions Limited; p19tl © Underwood & Underwood/Corbis; p19tr, p19b © Mary Evans Picture Library/Onslow Auctions Limited; p19m © Bettmann/Corbis. **p20-21 Iceberg, right ahead!**: p21b (*Titanic* distress message in timeline) © The National Archives UK (DN #10393); **p22-23 Abandon ship**: p22tl © Image Asset Management Ltd./SuperStock; p22m © Mary Evans Picture Library/Alamy; p22bl © Illustrated London News Ltd./Mary Evans; p23t © National Museums Northern Ireland Collection, Harland and Wolff, Ulster Folk and Transport Museum; p23ml © The National Archives/Heritage Images/TopFoto; p23mr (life buoy) © Mary Evans Picture Library/Onslow Auctions Limited; p23b © The Granger Collection/TopFoto; **p24-25 *Carpathia* to the rescue**: p24t © The National Archives/Heritage Images; p24m © Illustrated London News Ltd./Mary Evans; p24b © Mary Evans Picture Library/Alamy; p25tl © Roger-Viollet/Rex Features; p25tr © The Print Collector/Alamy; p25m © The Granger Collection/TopFoto; p25b © Richard Gardner/Rex Features; **p26-27 The aftermath**: p26t, p26b © Illustrated London News Ltd./Mary Evans; p26m © Underwood & Underwood/Corbis; p27t, p27m © Mary Evans Picture Library/Onslow Auctions Limited; p27b © Lake County Museum/Corbis; **p28-29 Passenger stories**: p28t © Bettmann/Corbis; p28m © Bettmann/Corbis; p28b © V&A Images; p29tl © Randy Bryan Bigham; p29tr © National Maritime Museum, Greenwich, UK, Lord-MacQuitty Collection; p29m © Archive Pics/Alamy; p29bl, p29br Phil Yeomans/Rex Features; **p30-31 Discovering the wreck**: p30bl © Emory Kristof/National Geographic Stock; p30br © Disney/Everett/Rex Features; p31t, p31m © Ralph White/Corbis; p31bl © Peter Brooker/Rex Features; p31br © Emory Kristof/National Geographic Stock

Edited by Ruth Brocklehurst and Rachel Firth

Additional design by Lucy Wain, Emily Barden, Brian Voakes, Emily Beevers and Sam Chandler

With thanks to Ruth King

Digital manipulation by John Russell and Nick Wakeford